Dear
Nanny,

We just wanted to let
you know how much we
Love You!

♡ ♡ ♡ ♡ ♡ ♡

Mickey, Matt
and Kelly

*A* grandmother is the one person in the world
who loves you with all her heart,
who remembers the child you were
and cherishes the person
you've become.

— Barbara Cage

# A Grandmother's Love Is Forever

A Blue Mountain Arts® Collection
Celebrating the Special Place
a Grandmother Holds in Our Hearts

Edited by Diane Mastromarino

**Blue Mountain Press**™

SPS Studios, Inc., Boulder, Colorado

We wish to thank Susan Polis Schutz for permission to reprint the following poems that appear in this publication: "Older people could teach us..." and "Grandmothers play games with their grandchildren...." Copyright © 1982, 1984 by Stephen Schutz and Susan Polis Schutz. All rights reserved.

ISBN: 0-88396-679-4

ACKNOWLEDGMENTS appear on page 64.

Certain trademarks are used under license.

Manufactured in China.
First Printing: June 2002

 This book is printed on recycled paper.

This book is printed on fine quality, laid embossed, 80 lb. paper. This paper has been specially produced to be acid free (neutral pH) and contains no groundwood or unbleached pulp. It conforms with all the requirements of the American National Standards Institute, Inc., so as to ensure that this book will last and be enjoyed by future generations.

# SPS Studios, Inc.

P.O. Box 4549, Boulder, Colorado 80306

# Contents

# Grandmothers Are Really Angels Sent from Heaven

Grandmothers are angels
sent down from heaven
to keep watch
over their families
as they grow.
They are angels
who touch the hearts of
each and every person they meet
with their special words
      of wisdom
and gentle understanding.
Grandmothers are angels
who know how to listen;
they give advice and direction
by sharing the history
of their lives.
They have a powerful influence
on their families.
With every smile that they share
and all the love they give,
grandmothers are a unique
      and wonderful part
of our lives.

— Laura Medley

# I Feel So Lucky to Have You for My Grandma

As far back as I can remember,
we have shared special times, warm hugs,
pats on the back, special looks, smiles, and
a hand to hold.
You have always made me feel important
and loved.
You are quick to share laughter and fun,
and some of my best times
have been with you.
Some people might say that you spoil me,
and maybe in some ways you do,
but you're tough, too.

You believe in my talents and abilities
and expect me to try, to do, and to be
my best.
Even then, your expectations
never exceed what I'm capable of,
and I appreciate that my best is always
good enough for you.
I love you, Grandma, and I want to
thank you
for sharing your life — and your love —
with me.

— Barbara Cage

# You Are an Extraordinary Grandmother

Even before I ask,
you're always there for me —
to comfort and to heal me,
to touch and to bless me.
You are so special.
You've brought hope into every situation
and growth into every new challenge.
You've been a shoulder to lean on,
a heart to rely on,
and a voice to cheer me on.
Thank you for sharing yourself,
for the offerings of time
    and conversation.
Thank you for your thoughtfulness,
    your caring,
and the touch of your hand
    holding mine tighter.
Thank you for all that you are,
    all that you do,
and all that you have been to me.

— Linda E. Knight

11

# One Thing Will Never Change

Life is so unpredictable. Changes always come along... in big ways and small steps, sometimes giving us a little nudge and other times turning our whole world upside down. So many changes; some subtle and almost unnoticeable, some drastic and more difficult to deal with.

But throughout all of life's changing and rearranging, I'm so glad that
    there is one wonderful thing
       that will never change...

In the passing of life's moments, I know that yesterday is already gone and that tomorrow will soon be here. The one thing I will take with me in all the days that lie ahead... is the one thing that has seen me through so many times in the past.
    It's something that will never change.

You are such a steady, strong, and beautiful part
of my life. You never cease to amaze me with
the constancy of your giving, the unselfishness
of your heart, and the reassurance of your smile.

And I thought it would be nice just to let you
know that my special feelings for you are going
to last forever and ever and ever.

— Marta Best

# I Appreciate You...
# for All that You Do

You always find time to listen;
you always find room in your heart.
You are always there with a hug.
Some people talk about being generous,
    kind, and loving.
You embody all these things,
but I don't think I've ever heard you
talk about this,
not even once.

You are a great source of comfort
to those you love,
and I feel so blessed to know you.
Sometimes we forget to say
"thank you" to the people
who brighten our day
with their presence.
We forget to tell them how much
all they do and all they are
really mean to us.
So I just wanted to say "thanks"
for being you and standing by me.
Thank you for everything.

— Tim Douglas Jensen

# A Grandmother Teaches Us So Much

---

The experience
In her hands alone
Is enough to fill a lifetime.
She has lived through history,
Eras of days gone by.
She has seen many inventions,
Watched some come and some go,
Just as she's seen people come and go.
She's watched the passing of history,
Witnessed the birth of new generations.
Her years have brought her wisdom
That she so generously shares.

— Kimberly Woods

How very wide your circle is, dear Grandma, all around you and so far! Our family is due to you, our happiness — because you did it in your family.... So many things we love are you, I can't seem to explain except by little things, but flowers and beautiful handmade things — small stitches. So much of our reading and thinking — so many sweet customs and so much of our... well, our religion. It is all you. I hadn't realized it before. This is so vague but do you see a little, dear Grandma? I want to thank you.

— Anne Morrow Lindbergh

Older people
could teach us
so much
if we would
only listen
Their wisdom
their simplicity
their experiences
their many years of living
We need them to
live with us
with our families
to teach us
and our children
all they know
to love us
and to let us
love them
and to let us
help them
when they
need it
A family
is not complete
without its
eldest
members

— Susan Polis Schutz

# Grandma, I Hope to Be like You Someday

You are someone
I look up to
someone I try to model
my life after
I have learned so much
from your past —
from your wonderful stories
about growing up
and growing older
and about
the way things used to be

You have helped me pave
my own roads
with your wisdom
and thoughtful guidance
and because of that
I feel very confident
in the choices I make
and in the paths
I choose to follow
I feel lucky to have you
in my life
and so very proud
to be your grandchild

— Elle Mastro

*Y*our caring heart has carried me to heights I alone
     could never reach.
You have been my greatest inspiration,
     my guiding light.
You have brought me to places in time
     I otherwise would not be a part of.
Through your past, I have learned so much
     about who I am, about where I come from,
     even where I may be headed.
Your wonderful advice has served as a guide for me;
     your wisdom and experience have been my teacher.
Your kindness and compassion warm my heart,
     reminding me that I will never be alone.
From you, I have learned to reach, to dare, to dream,
     to live my life to the fullest extent.
You have given so much of yourself to me, and
     I only hope I can use it to become all that you are.
For all this, for all you've done,
     for your presence in my life,
     Grandmother, I thank you.

— Diane Mastromarino

# There Are So Many Things That Make My Grandmother Special

*A* **smile** that permeates my heart and lifts my spirits on a dreary day, leaving me feeling valued beyond measure.

Gentle and steady **eyes** that selflessly and uncritically gaze in my direction, always seeing the inner beauty and true person in me.

Sensitive **ears** that listen proudly to my dreams and desires, patiently to my rambling anecdotes, and reassuringly to my concerns and fears.

**Lips** that profess a sincere love for me — ones that compliment and praise me continuously and can be counted on to tell the truth.

Loving **arms** that embrace me tightly and never let me go without a comforting pat on the back. Arms that tirelessly prepare a favorite ice-cream dessert on special occasions.

Steady **hands** that can fasten a button or tie a shoelace at a moment's notice, applaud my successes, and never forget to wave goodbye from the window.

A sharp and powerful **mind** that is able to remember intricate details and recount numerous stories of days gone by.

A discerning **spirit** that is able to see through the haze and get right to the heart of the matter, offering wisdom, advice, and consolation.

A joyful **heart** that is accepting of my faults, yet genuinely nurturing and unconditionally loving.

I wish to be like you, Grandmother.
I love you dearly...
and I thank you for loving me.

— Kimberly W. Shakelton

# No One Could Ever Replace You in My Life

*A* grandmother as essential as you is so much more than a part of my history. You are such a beautiful part of my present, too, and a hopeful part of every horizon I look forward to. You're always in my heart, cheering me up over the miles, encouraging me with your example, and — as usual — being more dear to me than my words can say. You have a very unique and important role in my life, and no one can ever take your place with me. The love I have for you is in the most special place in my heart, and it always — <u>always</u> — will be.

I don't think many people ever have the chance to be as blessed as I have been. You have contributed so much to my beliefs, my wisdom, my perspectives, my impressions of how to turn stumbling blocks into steppingstones, and to my knowledge of the sanctity of family ties and the treasures that are found in happy homes.

I'm so glad you're my grandmother. If I had been given the chance to choose, I would have told God I just wanted the most wonderful grandmother in the world,
and I know He would have
given me you.

— Emilia Larson

# A Grandmother's Love Is Unconditional

*M*y grandmother was the one who was always there for me. It never seemed to matter to her what I had done, whom I might have offended, or how I planned to fix my transgression. In my young mind, these events were earth-shattering catastrophes with tremendous consequences; to her, they were no more urgent than scattered clouds that temporarily block the sun on a fine summer afternoon.

Not until many years later, when life's path had led me through experiences I could never have imagined as I sat there in Grandma's kitchen, did I realize the source of her calm assurance in the midst of crisis, and her confidence "that everything works out for the best." It was <u>perspective</u>.

By virtue of her years, with all their attendant joys, griefs, hardships, and celebrations, she was able to take the "long view" of everything, both good and bad. It gave her great inner strength, and an appreciation for the rhythms of life that younger people — even my parents — did not possess.

As a child, I did not have words for it, but I instinctively gravitated to it as a ship at sea aims for the lighthouse beam. Even then, I knew it was the greatest gift I would ever receive: my grandmother's unconditional love.

— Noble Halloway

# What Is a Grandma?

A grandma is warm hugs
   and sweet memories.
She remembers all your accomplishments
and forgets all your mistakes.
She is someone you can tell
   your secrets and worries to,
and she hopes and prays that
   all your dreams come true.
She always loves you,
   no matter what.
She can see past temper tantrums
   and bad moods,
and makes it clear that they
   don't affect how precious
     you are to her.
She is an encouraging word
   and a tender touch.
She is full of proud smiles.
She is the one person in the world
   who loves you with all her heart,
who remembers the child you were
and cherishes the person
   you've become.

             — Barbara Cage

# Grandmothers

---

*If* you want to know the meaning of "grandmother,"
don't go to a dictionary. Instead, look into the hearts of
young children everywhere. You'll find that "grandmother"
and "love" have the exact same definition.

— Webster St. James

*Grandma* was a kind of first-aid station, or a Red Cross
nurse, who took up where the battle ended, accepting
us and our little sobbing sins, gathering the whole of
us into her lap, restoring us to health and confidence
by her amazing faith in life and in a mortal's strength
to meet it.

— Lillian Smith

*A* grandmother's love
is sunshine for the soul
and a source of warmth
and memories.

— Linda E. Knight

$\mathcal{T}$o small children,
grandmothers are warm hugs,
cookies, teddy bears, and
smiling faces who always
listen and take you seriously
when you talk about
the monster under the bed
or your invisible friend.

— Patricia A. Teckelt


$\mathcal{A}$ grandmother is the only person... that can stick
her finger down someone's throat, look up their
behind, or give them a bath... and it's okay.

— Arthur Kornhaber, M.D.


$\mathcal{A}$ grandmother is... a little like a magician. She can gather
the threads of any ordinary day and with them weave a
tapestry of laughter and love and memories that stays in
your heart always.

— Stella Lloyd

# A Great Big
# Thank-You

Thank you for taking the hours
out of your own precious days
to make a little more sunlight shine in mine.

Thank you for being a generous soul
and a beautiful spirit
in a world that could use
a million more people just like you.

Thanks so much for everything you've done
and for all that you
continue to do.

— J. Kalispell

# Home Is My Special Memory of You

─── ❧ ───

You can no more measure a home by inches,
or weigh it by ounces, than you can set up
the boundaries of a summer breeze, or calculate
the fragrance of a rose. Home is the love which
is in it.

— Edward Whiting

If you wanted to gather up all tender memories, all
lights and shadows of the heart, all banquetings and
reunions... and had only just four letters with which to
spell out that height and depth and length and breadth
and magnitude and eternity of meaning, you would
write it all out with these four capital letters: H-O-M-E.

— T. De Witt Talmage

*It's the inside of a house
that makes it a home.
It's not furnishings or décor,
but the family photo albums
filled with loving memories.
Home is the people who gather
at dinnertime,
the cozy atmosphere of talk and laughter,
and the informality of sharing
everything together.
It's the privilege of having
friendship close by
and being loved despite
your faults;
it's the deepest level of understanding,
the highest peak of caring,
and being part of something
so unique.
There's no greater place on earth
than the inside of a house
filled with those who make home
everything it's meant to be.
It's where memories are made
from the warmth of smiles,
spontaneous hugs, caring hugs,
and those who are remembered
with love.
Home is my special memory of you.*

— Barbara J. Hall

# When the Grandchildren Visit

The house is ready for them

I have milk and cookies
There are games and toys
Fragile objects are put away
Flower vases are removed

They're here

Cheerful and noisy
they fill the rooms with motion
It's a whirlwind of excitement
We sing and play
We kiss and hug
They leave with presents

They're gone
The house is empty without them

But the house is ready
for me —
with mud on the rugs
jam on the chairs
wet towels on the floor
one shoe under the couch
half-eaten candy in an ashtray
a traumatized dog
and one exhausted
grandmother

— Natasha Josefowitz, Ph.D.

# The Magic of a Grandma's Love Touches Your Life like Nothing Else Can

The magic of a grandma
is the way she
can put a smile on your face
when no one else can
and make any cloudy day disappear.

The magic of a grandma
is the way she
can share her words of wisdom
and fill your heart
with many happy memories.

The magic of a grandma
is the way she
can give you encouragement
and fill you to overflowing
with the confidence you need.

The magic of a grandma
is the way she
can give you all her love
and make you feel like
the most important person
in the world.

The magic of a grandma
is the way she
can help build your faith
and teach you patience
at the same time.

The magic of a grandma
is the way she
can make you feel
proud to be a part
of the same family she is,
and blessed
to have her as your grandma.

— Karen Richey

# Grandma, You Are an Angel

All these years, you've tucked
   away your wings
behind the kindness of your smile
and the tenderness of your heart.
I've always known that you were
   extraordinary,
and now I see that all along
you've been an angel in disguise.

— Deana Marino

*S*ometimes you are lucky enough
to experience (and recognize)
a glimpse of the light that is
Knowledge and Love
in the purest of forms,
and an unseen hand pauses
to touch your brow
and smooth away uncertainty
    and fear.
Some of us call this hand
    an angel.

When an angel touches you,
you are left with
a feeling of peace,
a message of hope,
and a brighter life.

I want to thank you
for being one of the angels
who has alighted upon my spirit
and blessed my life.

— Gina Breitkreutz

# A Grandmother's Smile

When a grandmother smiles,
You can see her childhood,
Her youth,
And her now-humorous heartaches.

You see, shining faintly around her,
The glimmer of growing up
And heartaches becoming
    painfully real.

Behind her smile is the beginning
    of wisdom
Learned from youth,
The getting up and trying again,
The laughter.

You see the past that began to shape her
    into what she is today —
Marriage,
Childbirth,
Still growing up over and over again,
Thinking you've gotten it down
    and then starting over.

There is joy behind her smile,
Tears, and so many memories.

She remembers the point in her life
     when she had to decide
Whether to start looking back on
     it all,
Or keep looking forward forever.
Then came her grandchildren —
More joy, more tears, more memories —
And she began to realize that life
     holds something for you
Around every corner.

When a grandmother smiles,
     you can see her heart.

— Laura E. Wiginton

# A Hug
# for You, Grandma

Sometimes it's nice
to get an unexpected hug
for no other reason than just
because you're loved and cared for.
It's a good feeling to know that
simply because you're you,
someone wants to show you
how much you mean to them.

So while you're reading these words,
don't think of them as just words...

Think of each one
as a hug
for your heart
from mine!

— Barbara J. Hall

# Young at Heart Forever

———— ❧ ————

*A*ge should be measured not only by years. It should be weighted by the enthusiasm generated after youth, the involvement perpetuated beyond middle life, and the dreams initiated and realized during retirement. Some will remain forever young.

— Edith Schaffer Lederberg

## Inside Out

*N*o matter how old I am on the outside
I am twenty years younger inside

My wrinkled skin covers a youthful one
my grey hair recalls being red

My heavier shape hides a lithe, slender body
my slower step remembers
having a spring in it

No matter how old I am on the outside
there is a vibrant, young woman inside

— Natasha Josefowitz, Ph.D.

*N*ow here we are, you and I, ready to take on one more slice of life. But we are still girls. Deep inside us, warm and cherished, is the same person who has done the best she could through whatever came into her life. The face is changed. But the Girl is here — the Girl with the Grandmother Face, and the whole world is gonna be glad we're still around.

— Frances Weaver

*A*s long as my hands
can build sandcastles
and I can sing lullabies
and tell bedtime stories
As long as I can dance
ring around the rosey
and pull candies from my pockets
As long as I can bake cookies
and color rainbows, moons, and stars —

I will remain 40 - 60 - 80 years young
and my heart and my grandchild agree

— Deana Marino

# Grandma, You Are Everything to Me

My grandma gives so much
with her loving words and kind praise
She always finds the words
to make things right
She is a feeling of warmth
serenity and love within my heart
She is a source of joy and happiness
She was with me through the days
when I was little, staying by my side
to make sure I was okay
She gave me so much of what I needed
and has made me so much
of who I am today
The times she held my hand
and walked me through my days
meant so much to me
Grandma, you are sweet memories
of joy and love and kindness
and a symbol of all that is dear
You are the essence
of all that makes our family special
You hold treasured memories
of years gone by
and you hope for only the best in the future
You love me wholeheartedly
and have found a special place in my heart
For all the love you've shared
you are loved far more
than these words can convey

— Shannon M. Lester

# The Difference Between Parents and Grandparents

---- ❧ ----

*The* nice thing about grandparents...
they can love you wholeheartedly
without the discipline and the
conflicts that you have with your
own parents.

— Martina Navratilova

*As* parents we could never stand back.... We were too
close, too involved. As grandparents, however close and
involved we may be, we still have that precious modicum
of detachment that comes with being the older generation.
We are already standing back a step, and we have the
perspective from which to watch the seeds of character
yielding up their secrets.

— Ruth Goode

$\mathcal{W}$hat a lonely world this would be
    if there were no grandmothers!
Who else could we turn to
when our parents seem far too busy
and we need a jar to hold a bug in
or an audience to laugh at a joke
    we just made up
or a big lap to crawl in when
    someone's mean to us?
Where else could we go
    when we're looking for a place
that feels even more like "home"
    than our own house?
Grandmothers are the ones who
    make this world beautiful
with countless, unselfish acts of love.

— Spenser Chapman

Grandmothers play games
with their grandchildren
that parents would never play
Grandmothers take their grandchildren
to places that parents
would not think of
Grandmothers give their grandchildren
an understanding of heritage
that the parents cannot give
Grandmothers and grandchildren
frolic in happiness in each other's presence
I am so glad
that I am able to
have this wonderful, unique and
beautiful
relationship
with you
I love you

— Susan Polis Schutz

# The Heart That Binds the Family Together

---------- ❧ ----------

*A* grandmother is the foundation upon which the world's strongest and closest families are built. Her love and loyalty hold together a collection of individuals that might otherwise fly apart on the tides of change and time.

— Franklin Morganfeld

*S*he's part of the cement
That holds a family together.
Listening to her stories
Introduces us to our ancestors.
The ways in which
She's touched our lives
Will remain with us
Forever,
Just as she will remain
In our thoughts,
Our stories,
Our children,
Our family,
Our lives.

— Kimberly Woods

*You* are always there in the center of our family.
When disagreements, hurt feelings, and distance
separate us from each other and weaken the bonds
between us, there is still one thing we all have in
common. Everyone turns to you for understanding,
sympathy, and love... and we always find it there,
waiting patiently for us.

— Grant Lee


*The* happiness that families share is the
greatest joy in the world. The knowledge
that there is always someone who cares
is a treasure nothing can match. The love
of a family makes life beautiful.

— Andrew Harding Allen

# To My Very Special Grandma

"Special" is a word that is used
to describe something one-of-a-kind
like a hug or a sunset
or a person who spreads love
with a smile or kind gesture.
"Special" describes people
who act from the heart
and keep in mind the hearts of others.
"Special" applies to something
that is admired and precious
and which can never be replaced.
"Special" is the word that best
describes you.

— Teri Fernandez

# The Bond Between Grandmother and Grandchild

——————————— ❧ ———————————

The old and the young are fascinated by one another. A grandmother can sit on a park bench for hours, transfixed, watching her grandchild at play. The child, aware of grandmother's undivided attention, delights in performing for an audience of one.

— Arthur Kornhaber, M.D., and Kenneth L. Woodward

A grandmother is the brightest star
in the world of any grandchild.

— McKinley Smithfield

As I grow up and you grow older
we share our lives
you giving me your past
as I in return speak of a present
you try your best to understand
You hold my hands inside your own
I hold you inside my heart, always

— Diane Mastromarino

$G$randchildren... rekindle for us the spirit of play, the child's sense of adventure and discovery. Grandparents are always being told that they are living history to their grandchildren, that they give the children the reassurance of their roots, the strengthening awareness of continuity. For me and many grandmothers I have talked to, it works the other way as well. They give us continuity. They link us to our own motherhood and childhood years, to our parents and grandparents and the stories we remember of times even earlier than those. And they link us to the future as well. They give us a vested interest in the world in which they will live. They make us aware of the world in which we are living today and helping to create for tomorrow.

— Ruth Goode

# You Are an Inspiration to Me

I celebrate your life, Grandma.
Not the years or the days,
but all the mountains
you have climbed,
all the rivers
you have crossed,
the rise of your chin above
the water when the fast-moving
current of life caught you unaware.
You are always looking upward —
it is obvious by
the smile
on your face
and the strength
of your hand as you
reach out for the shoreline,
determined to stand
firm again on solid ground.
You have journeyed
the path of a woman,
tasted its sweet delight,
known its bitter struggle.
You have lived life,
and you have given life.
You are truly a remarkable woman.

— Patricia Ann Doneson

# Thank You for Everything You Do for Me

*I* thank you. So much.
My thoughts thank you.
My smile thanks you.
And my brighter days thank you.

Thank you.
For making more than a difference.
For taking more than just the time.
Thank you for doing... all that you
so wonderfully do.

I wish I could express the gratitude
I feel in so many different ways.
It's hard to say the meaningful things;
the words that come to mind
usually find themselves falling short
of the feelings that I'd like to share
and the things I'd like to say.
But I want you to know that
"thanks" is one emotion
that flows directly into the heart.

And it's a very wonderful feeling
that never goes away.

— Casey Whilson

# A Grandmother's Love
## Is Forever

A grandmother's love is the sun that shines the brightest memories upon you. It is a promise of beautiful moments to come that will warm your heart for the rest of your days.

A grandmother's love is the radiance of her pride in who you are. It is a warm assurance that you have a best friend and a special supporter everywhere you go — someone who knows what's important to you and who believes that you can do anything you desire. Her love is a guiding light to help you find your way. It will take you to the place where your dreams lie and your potential can be reached.

Her love shines with the wisest teachings. It is the warmth of arms to hold you, the golden voice that calls your name. It is the healing power of the best medicine for every ache and pain of body and soul. It is the sun that glows inside of you to match the brightness of her smiles. It is joy and comfort that spreads for miles.

A grandmother's love is the light that kindles all types of kindness. It inspires words and deeds that are gentle, helpful, and uplifting. It is just what the world needs. It is the spirit of unselfish giving and positive living, filled with the richness of wisdom and experience.

A grandmother's love is the sun that shines for you with pride, joy, and a guiding light that will forever touch your life with smiles.

— Jacqueline Schiff

# ACKNOWLEDGMENTS

The following is a partial list of authors whom the publisher especially wishes to thank for permission to reprint their works.

Tim Douglas Jensen for "I Appreciate You... for All that You Do." Copyright © 2002 by Tim Douglas Jensen. All rights reserved.

Kimberly Woods for "The experience in her hands alone..." and "She's part of the cement...." Copyright © 2002 by Kimberly Woods. All rights reserved.

Hartcourt, Inc., and The Lindbergh Foundation for "How very wide..." from BRING ME A UNICORN: DIARIES AND LETTERS OF ANNE MORROW LINDBERGH 1922-1928. Copyright © 1972 by Anne Morrow Lindbergh. All rights reserved.

Kimberly W. Shakelton for "There Are So Many Things That Make My Grandmother Special." Copyright © 2002 by Kimberly W. Shakelton. All rights reserved.

Linda E. Knight for "A grandmother's love is sunshine...." Copyright © 2002 by Linda E. Knight. All rights reserved.

Patricia A. Teckelt for "To small children,..." Copyright © 2002 by Patricia A. Teckelt. All rights reserved.

Arthur Kornhaber, M.D. for "A grandmother is the only person..." from BETWEEN PARENTS AND GRANDPARENTS, published by St. Martin's Press LLC. Copyright © 1986 by Arthur Kornhaber, M.D.

Barbara J. Hall for "It's the inside of a house...." Copyright © 2002 by Barbara J. Hall. All rights reserved.

Laura E. Wiginton for "A Grandmother's Smile." Copyright © 2002 by Laura E. Wiginton. All rights reserved.

Edith Schaffer Lederberg for "Age should be measured...." Copyright © 2002 by Edith Schaffer Lederberg. All rights reserved.

Hyperion, for "Now here we are..." from THE GIRLS WITH THE GRANDMOTHER FACES by Frances Weaver. Copyright © 1996 by Frances Weaver. All rights reserved.

Shannon M. Lester for "Grandma, You Are Everything to Me." Copyright © 2002 by Shannon M. Lester. All rights reserved.

Alfred E. Knopf, a division of Random House, Inc., for "The nice thing about grandparents..." from MARTINA: AUTOBIOGRAPHY by Martina Navratilova and George Vecsey. Copyright © 1985 by Martina Enterprises, Inc. All rights reserved.

McGraw-Hill, Inc., for "As parents we could..." and "Grandchildren rekindle..." from A BOOK FOR GRANDMOTHERS by Ruth Goode. Copyright © 1976 by Ruth Goode. All rights reserved.

Curtis Brown, Ltd., for "The old and the young..." from GRANDPARENTS / GRANDCHILDREN: THE VITAL CONNECTION by Arthur Kornhaber, M.D., and Kenneth L. Woodward. Copyright © 1981 by Arthur Kornhaber and Kenneth L. Woodward. All rights reserved.

Patricia Ann Doneson for "You Are an Inspiration to Me." Copyright © 2002 by Patricia Ann Doneson. All rights reserved.

Jacqueline Schiff for "A Grandmother's Love Is Forever." Copyright © 2002 by Jacqueline Schiff. All rights reserved.

A careful effort has been made to trace the ownership of poems used in this anthology in order to obtain permission to reprint copyrighted materials and give proper credit to the copyright owners. If any error or omission has occurred, it is completely inadvertent, and we would like to make corrections in future editions provided that written notification is made to the publisher:

SPS STUDIOS, INC., P.O. Box 4549, Boulder, Colorado 80306.